GROWTH
GUIDES
for Adults

Forgiven
Experience
the Surprising
Grace of God

JOSH McDOWELL
SEAN McDOWELL

HARVEST HOUSE PUBLISHERS
EUGENE, OREGON

Cover by Koechel Peterson & Associates, Inc., Minneapolis, Minnesota

Cover photo © Hemera / Thinkstock

THE UNSHAKABLE TRUTH is a trademark of The Hawkins Children's LLC. Harvest House Publishers, Inc., is the exclusive licensee of the federally registered trademark THE UNSHAKABLE TRUTH.

FORGIVEN—EXPERIENCE THE SURPRISING GRACE OF GOD
Course 6 of The Unshakable Truth® Journey Growth Guides
Copyright © 2012 by Josh McDowell Ministry and Sean McDowell
Published by Harvest House Publishers
Eugene, Oregon 97402
www.harvesthousepublishers.com

ISBN 978-0-7369-4345-1 (pbk.)
ISBN 978-0-7369-4346-8 (eBook)

Printed in the United States of America

12 13 14 15 16 17 18 19 20 / VP-NI / 10 9 8 7 6 5 4 3 2 1

CONTENTS

About the Authors

Authors Josh and Sean McDowell collab-orated with their writer to bring you this Unshakable Truth Journey course. The content is based upon Scripture and the McDowells' book *The Unshakable Truth*.

Over 50-plus years, **Josh McDowell** has spoken to more than 10 million people in 120 countries about the evidence for Christianity and the difference the Chris-tian faith makes in the world. He has authored or coauthored more than 120 books (with more than 51 million copies in print), including such classics as *More Than a Carpenter* and *New Evidence That Demands a Verdict*.

Sean McDowell is an educator and a popular speaker at schools, churches, and conferences nationwide. He is author of *Ethix: Being Bold in a Whatever World*, coauthor of *Understanding Intelligent Design*, and general editor of *Apologetics for a New Generation* and *The Apologetics Study Bible for Students*. He is currently pursuing a PhD in apologetics and worldview studies. Sean's website, www.seanmcdowell.org, offers his blog, many articles and videos, and much additional curriculum.

About the Writer

Dave Bellis is a ministry consultant focusing on ministry planning and product development. He is a writer, producer, and product developer. He and his wife, Becky, have two grown children and live in northeastern Ohio.

Acknowledgments

We would like to thank the many people who brought creativity and insight to forming this course:

Terri Snead and David Ferguson of Great Commandment Network for their writing insights for the TruthTalk and Truth Encounter sections of this growth guide.

Terry Glaspey for his insights and guidance as he helped in the development of the Unshakable Truth Journey concept.

Paul Gossard for his skillful editing of this manuscript.

And finally, the entire team at Harvest House, who graciously endured the process with us.

Josh McDowell
Sean McDowell
Dave Bellis

What Is the Unshakable Truth Journey All About?

You hear people talk about having a personal relationship with God and knowing Christ. But what does that really mean? Sure, they probably are saying they are a Christian and God has personally forgiven them of their sins. But is that all of what being a Christian really is—being a person forgiven by God?

We are here to say that being a follower of Christ is much, much more than that. Everything you are and what you are becoming as a person is wrapped up in it. When Jesus said he was "the way, the truth, and the life" (John 14:6) he was offering us a supernatural way to follow in his way, his truth, and his life. As we do, we begin to understand what we were meant to know and be and how we were meant to live. Actually, when we become a follower of Christ we begin to take on Jesus' view of the world and begin to think like and be motivated like and live like Christ. And that brings incredible joy and satisfaction to life.

So when we see life and relationships as Jesus sees them, we begin to get a clear picture of who we are and discover our true identity. We begin to realize why we are here and recognize our purpose and meaning in life. We begin to know where we are going and experience our destiny and mission in a life larger than ourselves. Being a Christian—a committed follower of Christ—unlocks our identity, purpose, and destiny in life. It is then that the natural process of spiritual reproduction takes place. That is when imparting the faith to our family and others around us becomes a reality. But what is involved in being that kind of a follower of Christ—a person who has joy and satisfaction in life and knows how to effectively impart the faith to the next generation?

The Unshakable Truth Journey gets to the core of what being a true follower of Christ means and what knowing Christ is all about. Together you and your group will begin a journey that will last a lifetime. It is a journey into what you as a follower of Christ are to believe biblically, how you process your beliefs into core values, and how you live them out in all your relationships. In fact, we will take the core truths of Christianity and break them down into a five-step process:

1. ***What truths do you as a Christian believe biblically?***

   In the first step you and your group will interact with what we as Christians believe about God, his Word, and so on.

2. ***Why do you believe those truths?***

   Sure, you can say you believe certain truths because they are biblical, but when you know *why* they are true it grounds you in your faith. Additionally, it gives you confidence to pass them on to others—especially your family.

3. ***How are these truths relevant to life?***

   In many respects truth isn't very meaningful until you see how it is relevant to your own life.

4. ***How do you live these truths out personally?***

   Knowing how the truth of Christianity is relevant is necessary, but what it leads to is understanding how that truth is to become a living reality in your own life. That's where the rubber meets the road, so to speak.

5. ***How do you, as a group, live these truths out before your community and world?***

   As Christians we are all to be "salt" and "light" to

the world around us. In this step you and your group will discover how to impact your own community with truth that is lived out corporately—as a body.

Be warned! The Unshakable Truth Journey isn't a program to study what Christianity is all about. Simply discovering what something is about has great limitations and ends up being of little value. Rather, this journey is about experiencing firsthand how God's truth is to be experienced in your life right now and, in fact, for the rest of your life. It's about knowing God's truth in a real, experiential way. The apostle John said, "It is by our actions that we know we are living in the truth" (1 John 3:19). You will be challenged repeatedly to increasingly know certain truths by experiencing them continually in your relationship with God and with those around you. It is then you will be able to pass on this ever-increasing faith journey to your family and friends.

There will be two specific exercises that appear throughout these courses. The first is entitled "Truth Encounter." This section is an invitation for you to stop and carefully reflect on the truth of each session. You'll be asked to encounter a truth of God as you relate personally with Jesus, as you live out the truth of God's Word with your small group, or as you relate personally with his people. Please don't rush past these Truth Encounters. They are designed to equip you in how to experience truth right in the room you're in!

The second exercise is an assignment for the week, called "TruthTalk." The TruthTalks are designed as conversation start-ers—ways to engage others in spiritual discussions. They will create opportunities for you to share what you've experienced in this course with others around you. This will help you com-municate God's truth with others as you share vulnerably about your own Unshakable Truth Journey.

What you discover here is to last a lifetime and beyond. You will never finish in this life nor in the life to come. God's truths are designed to be enjoyed forever. You see, experiencing God's truth and knowing him will grow throughout eternity, and your love of him will expand to contain it. And that process begins in the here and now. Your relationship with God may have begun 5 months, 5 years, or 50 years ago—it doesn't matter. The truths explored in these courses are to be applied at every level of life. And what is so encouraging is that while these truths are eter-nally deep they can be embraced and experienced by even a young child. That is the beauty and mystery of God's truth!

This particular Unshakable Truth Journey is one of 12 different growth guides. All the growth guides are based upon Josh and Sean McDowell's book *The Unshakable Truth*, which is the com-panion book to this course. The book covers 12 core truths of the Christian faith.

The growth guide you have in your hand covers the truth about the power of God's grace—how we actually obtain a relationship with God. Together we will explore how a right relationship with God is offered to us in spite of our sin. These five sessions lay the foundation for how to have a relationship with God and lead our families to that reality. Check out the other Unshakable Truth Journey courses in the back of this book.

Okay then, let our journey begin.

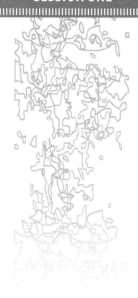

WHAT MAKES US RIGHT BEFORE GOD?

Did you ever have someone give you a significant gift or the privilege to do something when you weren't particularly deserving of it? Or have you given something significant to someone who wasn't very deserving? Tell of your experience, and particularly how you responded when receiving an undeserved gift or how the person responded to your gift.

_____

_____

_____

People often feel undeserving of gifts as if they must earn something to be worthy of the gift. Do you tend to feel you must earn what you get? Why or why not?

_____

_____

_____

OUR GROUP OBJECTIVE

To explore what we do and
what God does to make
us right before him.

Someone read Leviticus 6:2-5.

Restitution is a basic principle of Scripture—we are to repay those we have done wrong against. We have all sinned against God. Although Jesus paid for our salvation, do you feel you should do something on your part to, in a sense, pay restitution to God? Why or why not?

_____

_____

_____

Someone read Romans 3:27-28.

What is your justification (being declared right before God) *NOT* dependent on? Why?

_____

_____

_____

What *is* your justification, your being declared right before God, dependent upon? Why?

_____

_____

_____

Many people believe we are saved by faith. But actually Scripture teaches us that we are not declared right before God because of faith.

Someone read Ephesians 2:4-10.

This passage makes it clear how we are forgiven and made right before God. There is not something we do to earn it; it is by God's grace.

So what is faith all about? If we are saved by God's grace (his unmerited favor) then what does faith do for us?

_____

_____

_____

_____

_____

There is something we do to receive God's grace. We exercise faith in Jesus. And that faith in him acts as an arm that reaches out to receive God's merciful grace. And because of what Jesus did on the cross, we are forgiven and made right with God.

Someone read the following.

> The apostle Paul said, "I plead with you to give your bodies to God. Let them be a living and holy sacrifice—the kind he will accept. When you think of what he has done for you, is this too much to ask?" (Romans 12:1).

Jesus sacrificed his life for you. So must you give yourself as a living sacrifice in order for God to forgive you and make you his child? If not, how do you explain Romans 12:1?

_____

_____

_____

Jesus sacrificed himself and atoned for our sins. Because of his death and resurrection God redeems us. He has paid our debt and we are declared righteous before God. Then what do our deeds and giving of ourselves as a living sacrifice have to do with it all? Read Romans 3:21-28 and then Romans 7:4-6.

_____

_____

_____

_____

_____

Someone read the following.

Let's say you owed a mortgage on your house and it was a burdensome monthly payment. And suppose you got a free and clear title in the mail stating your debt was cancelled. To your surprise you learn that your uncle who lived in the area decided to pay your mortgage off. He did this completely out of the blue. In fact, you hadn't even talked to him for years, so it wasn't anything you said or did for him.

Question: Is there anything you can now do to further pay your debt to the mortgage company? Of course not. You no longer have a loan because it has been paid off. But while you can't do anything further to pay your debt, your heart is full of gratitude. So you reconnect with your uncle and say, "Thank you so much. I can't repay the mortgage payment—you did that out of mercy to me. But I want to do something. What can I do to show you my gratitude?" He explains that all he would like is to be closer to you. He wants to reconnect and be a closer family. You comply by including him in family functions and get-togethers.

This is a feeble illustration of the reality that we can do nothing to cancel our debt of sin. Nothing we can do earns us points with God. Out of a heart of grace he came, he died, and he rose again to purchase our salvation. We receive that salvation—our resurrected life in him—by faith in Jesus. Then out of a heart of gratitude we give our lives as a living sacrifice to him. And in this united relationship with him we live a life pleasing to God through the power of his Spirit. "Now we are united with the one who was raised from the dead. As a result, you can produce good fruit, this is, good deeds for God" (Romans 7:4).

So is there nothing we can say to God or do for God that would merit our redemption? Is there nothing we can do to earn our justification? Is there nothing we can leverage to acquire sanctification? Paul asked and answered those questions when he wrote:

> Can we boast then, that we have done anything to be accepted by God? No, because our acquittal is not based on our good deeds. It is based on our faith [in Jesus]. So we are made right with God through faith and not by obeying the law (Romans 3:27-28).

Performance-based people who want to earn what they get may find salvation by grace through faith hard to grasp, or at least hard to accept. But there is no human requirement to obtain God's offer of a relationship except to freely accept it. It is a gift based upon the requirements fulfilled by

Jesus. That is why when speaking of salvation Paul said, "It does not depend on the man who wills or the man who runs, but on God who has mercy" (Romans 9:16 NASB).

Therefore:

> **We believe the truth that being justified before God and cleansed of our sins is a result of God's grace through faith alone in Jesus as our sacrifice for sin.**

Christ atoned for our sin by his death on the cross. When we place our faith in him as our substitute, we are redeemed and justified before God. We are set apart as his holy people (sanctified). Not by what we have done, but because of what Christ has done. "Abraham believed God, and God counted him as righteous because of his faith. When people work, their wages are not a gift, but something they have earned. But people are counted as righteous not because of their work, but because of their faith in God who forgives sinners" (Romans 4:3-4).

Have you held some misconceptions or been slightly confused as to how we are saved? Have the ideas of grace and faith or justification and sanctification been unclear? Share where you have been in your thinking and where you are now.

_____

_____

_____

_____

_____

|||||||||||||||||||||||||||||||||||||||||||||||||||||||||||||||||||||||||||||||||||||||||||||||||||

Truth Encounter: A Meditation

Someone read Luke 7:36-38.

The following is designed as a meditation to help you reflect on Christ's redeeming love for the woman anointing Jesus' feet. Put yourself in the story as Jesus declares the woman's redemption and right standing before God. Put yourself in the story as Jesus contrasts the Pharisee's performance-based mentality with the woman's faith-filled acceptance of Christ's gift. Someone read the following aloud and meditate on this story:

> It was a bad idea from the start. What had made her think she could slip into the room unnoticed? The people drew away from her. Their hateful glares made her cheeks blaze behind her veil. No

matter how hard she tried to blend in, it seemed that her very presence provoked the worst in every crowd. The hushed whispers and muffled laughter stoked the embers of her anger. Did they think she was stupid? Did they think she did not know that the jokes were about her?

Simon, the host for this gathering, was the most important Pharisee in the village. Ceremoniously, he followed the visiting Teacher into the room, quickly scanning around to make sure that all was in order. His eyes quickly locked on the woman— what was she doing here?

For an intense moment, she endured his gaze. All ears strained in expectation of Simon's disgusted apology to his honored guest. The woman felt trapped, exposed. There was nothing to do but wait for Simon and his visitor to condemn her presence and her lifestyle. Her beating heart pounded as she stared at the floor. But no rebuke came.

Then she noticed the Teacher. *Why is he walking toward me?* she thought. Then she saw the look in his eyes. *He knows who I am!* she realized. *He knows what I have done! Why would he dare to come near me? Why doesn't he act like the others?* As the Teacher smiled at her, she suddenly realized that, for the first time since she was a little girl, she had met a Man who saw her as she wanted to be and not as she had become.

The woman began to cry. *I have been forgiven. I have been accepted. I have been cleansed*, she thought. She sank to her knees as tears poured from her eyes, seemingly washing away decades of sin and hurt. Her tears fell on the dusty, calloused feet of the Teacher.

The crowd fell silent; only her sobbing could be heard. Those in the room waited to see Simon's reaction. This Jesus was reported to be a prophet. But if he was, surely he would not allow himself to be approached by a common prostitute!

But Jesus did not move. His eyes ran with tears as well. Then the most amazing thing took place: Unashamedly, the woman removed her veil. Her dark hair cascaded onto the feet of Jesus, and she began to wash his feet and wipe them with her hair.

Her pocket held a small vial of perfume. She opened it, filling the air with a sweet aroma, and anointed the feet of the Teacher. Simon was filled with indignation. The Teacher's silence seemed to indicate his acceptance of the woman in spite of her sin. The flustered Pharisee demanded an explanation, and the Teacher replied.

"'Look at this woman kneeling here. When I entered your home, you didn't offer me water to wash the dust from my feet, but she has washed them with her tears and wiped them with her hair. You didn't give me a kiss of greeting, but she has kissed my feet again and again from the time I first came in. You neglected the courtesy of olive oil to anoint my head, but she has anointed my feet with rare perfume. I tell you, her sins—and they are many—have been forgiven, so she has shown me much love. But a person who is forgiven little shows only little love.' Then Jesus said to the woman, 'Your sins are forgiven'" (Luke 7:45-48).

How do you think this woman felt at that moment?

_____

_____

_____

Reflect on your sins being forgiven, the unconditional acceptance of the Savior, your being declared righteous before God. Consider singing a song of worship and praise to the Redeemer.

Break into groups of three or four and pray aloud with one another. Consider the following as your guide.

"Lord, as I reflect on your acceptance, forgiveness, redemption, and cleansing of me, my heart is moved with

_____. With faith, I receive your gifts, knowing that there is nothing I can do or say that could earn your gifts. Like the woman, I gratefully receive all that you have done on my behalf and I offer my humble thanks. You are a God who is worthy of our praise because _____
_____."

TruthTalk—An Assignment of the Week

Take time this week to share with a family member or friend what you have experienced in this session. Consider saying something like:

"No one can ever be made right in God's sight by doing what his law commands, for the more we know God's law, the clearer it becomes that we aren't obey-ing it. But now God

1 "I have a renewed gratitude for how Jesus has made things right between God and me. I am especially grateful for / amazed by God's…

_____
_____
_____
_____."

has shown us a different way of being right in his sight…. We are made right in God's sight when we trust in Jesus Christ [place our faith in him] to take away our sins…God in his gracious kindness [grace] declares us not guilty" (Romans 3:20-24). So by placing our faith in Jesus we are redeemed—purchased out of slavery; and justified—declared righteous before God.

2 "I used to think that I could work my way into pleasing God. I now have a different perspective and a really grateful heart. I'm amazed at God's gift of

_____ because…

_____

_____

_____

_____."

3 "I am so grateful for God's grace and understand a little more of his grace. I now "get" how God's grace is something he offers and gives. My role is to accept that gift by faith. Can I share more about how God is changing me? (Wait for response.) For example…

_____

_____

_____

_____."

Read chapter 25 of *The Unshakable Truth* book.

Close in Prayer

DOES CHRIST HAVE THE POWER TO SAVE US?

Review: How did your TruthTalk assignment go this week? What was the response?

_____

_____

_____

If you had the power to change things that you see as a problem in this world, what would that include?

_____

_____

_____

Someone read Isaiah 25:7-8.

God made a promise to the children of Israel and us that would eventually be fulfilled. What did the promise include?

_____
_____
_____

OUR GROUP OBJECTIVE

To gain a greater confidence that
Jesus has the power to save us as well
as granting us the power of prayer.

Someone read Romans 8:3.

Why can't obeying the law of Moses save us?

_____
_____
_____

What was God's plan in order to destroy sin's control over us?

_____
_____
_____

Someone read the following.

> Perhaps the greatest miracle of all was God becoming human in the form of Jesus, then sacrificing himself and raising from the dead to save us. So if

Jesus of Nazareth was truly the Son of God he no
doubt would have exhibited extraordinary power.
In fact, that would be a strong indicator that he *was*
God's Son.

Someone read John 5:36.

What did Jesus say his power to perform miracles indicated?

_____

_____

_____

Jesus clearly intended his miracles to be understood as a vali-
dation of his identity as God's Son. And as God's Son he was the
perfect sacrifice for our sin. But just what kind of miracles did
Jesus perform and what do they signify?

Someone read the passages below and then describe what
miracle Jesus performed.

Read Mark 4:39. Jesus _____

_____

Read Matthew 14:15-21. Jesus _____

_____

Read Mark 10:51-52. Jesus _____

_____

Read John 2:7-10. Jesus _____

_____

Read John 11:39-44. Jesus _____

_____

Who else but God has the mastery Jesus demonstrated over the human body, weather, food multiplication, chemistry, and even death itself? Who else but God's Son could do these things? Yet did Jesus do these things just to prove the point that he was the Son of God?

The performing of various miracles gives us an insight into the heart of God's Son. Something motivated Jesus to perform these miracles.

Jesus was present with the disciples in the midst of a storm, and he had promised they would go over to the other side. When the furious squall came up, Jesus calmed it (Mark 4:35-40). Why? What does this tell us about Jesus' interest in what the disciples were feeling?

_____

_____

_____

Why did Jesus feed the 5000 (Matthew 14)? What does this tell us about Jesus' heart interest? Why did he meet this need in the people?

_____

_____

_____

Why did Jesus heal the blind man (Mark 10)? What does this tell us about Jesus' heart interest? Why did he meet this need?

_____

_____

_____

Why did Jesus turn water into wine (John 2)? What does this tell us about Jesus' heart interest? Why did he meet the lack of the wedding party?

_____

_____

_____

Why did Jesus raise Lazarus from the dead (John 11)? What does this tell us about Jesus' heart interest? Why did he meet the desire of Mary and Martha?

_____

_____

_____

Read Matthew 9:36; 14:14; and 15:32.

There is a phrase or expression used in these verses and many more that most often describes Jesus' heart of love. What is it?

_____

Someone read the following.

> When Jesus saw the fear of the disciples because
> of the storm "he was moved with compassion."
> When he saw the sick he "was moved with compas-
> sion." When he saw those who were hungry he was
> "moved with compassion." When he saw a wedding
> party that had, to everyone's embarrassment, run
> out of wine, Christ was "moved with compassion."
>
> Sin and death has brought pain, suffering, and heart-
> ache to God's creation, and it has moved him with
> compassion. The miracles of Jesus are an indica-
> tor that he is not only our redeemer, but also our re-
> storer. He wants to restore broken hearts, broken
> bodies, hungry stomachs, fearful emotions, and even
> disappointed wedding planners. He is a miracle-
> working God who cares about us on every level.

Truth Encounter

Someone read Hebrews 13:8.

Reflect for a few moments on the truth of Christ's incredible
power combined with his compassionate heart. Since he is the
same yesterday, today, and forever, Jesus is still powerful and
still moved with compassion.

Like the disciples, are you experiencing storms and circumstances of life that have perhaps left you a little anxious and worried? Are you feeling a little overwhelmed or like life is out of control? Share your situation.

_____

_____

_____

Just as Jesus was moved with compassion for his disciples, his heart is moved with compassion for you. Christ is in effect saying to us: "Remember, your worry and your anxiety prompts my care. The God who calms storms is with you and cares for you. I am hoping that you'll trust in me."

Like the 5000 people on the hillside, are you in need of God's provision? Are you coming up short or empty-handed? Are there specific needs that only a miracle will provide? Explain.

_____

_____

_____

Just as Jesus was moved with compassion for the 5000, his heart is moved with compassion for you. Listen as he speaks to your heart and says, "The needs of your life prompt my care. I'm the God who feeds 5000 for dinner, and I care about the needs of your life."

Like the wedding party, do you need a God who is sensitive to the intricacies of relationships? Are there specific challenges in relationships in which you need God to intervene? Explain.

_____

_____

_____

Just as Jesus was moved with compassion for the wedding hosts, he feels compassion for you. The Savior's reassurance is available to you as he speaks to you: "Remember, I am sensitive and understand the relational nuances of your life. That's a part of why I came to this world, so you would know that I understand. My heart cares for you and is ready and responsive toward you, just as it was at the wedding."

Like Mary and Martha, do you need a God who is present and compassionate during the dark times of your life? Do you need to sense that he hasn't left you, been too busy for you, or forgotten you? Explain.

_____

_____

_____

Just as Jesus was moved with compassion for Mary and Martha (even though he knew of his plans to raise Lazarus from the dead), Christ is moved with compassion for you. Listen to him speak to you: "My heart feels deep compassion when you hurt. The pain of your heart fills my eyes with tears. I not only weep

for Mary and Martha, I weep for you. Be confident of my care.
Be reassured of my love."

Take the next few moments to share your response to the
scenes above with your group. Pray together. Tell Jesus about
your need for his intervention, provision, healing, involvement,
and care. Meditate on how Christ wants to interact with you, just
as he did with the people of the Gospels. Let his Spirit remind
you of Christ's care for you and how he shows you compassion.

Consider playing soft instrumental music as you meditate on
Jesus' care and compassion—just for you.

Next, pray with one or two others in your group, thanking God
for his compassionate response. Your prayers might sound like:

"God, I am so grateful for your compassion. I am especially
grateful that you see my need for _____
and you care. Remind me often of how your heart is moved
when you see my needs. Thank you for being a God who

_____

_____."

‖‖

Prayer: An Incredible Privilege

Someone read the following.

Not only do we have a God who cares for our needs directly, it is evident that God is at work through his people to bring a message of salvation and healing to a needy world. As his people, we have the privilege of joining him in prayer, faith, and trusting in the work of our sovereign God. As we remain Christ-centered with a focus on bringing him honor and glory, he will be pleased to answer our prayers.

Take a moment to reconsider the amazing, incredible privilege that we have been brought into a relationship with:

- the One who cares when we are anxious because of life's circumstances.

- the One who is interested and ready to provide for us when he sees our need.

- the One who sees our infirmities and need for healing and responds with compassion.

- the One who cares about our relationships with others around us and comes to our aid.

- the One who sees our pain and is moved with compassion himself.

This is the God we are able to come to in prayer!

Someone read James 4:2-3.

If we have a God who is all the things we have considered above, why don't we always get what we pray for?

_____

_____

Identify some prayer requests, specifically for your family, that God would be pleased to answer.

_____

_____

_____

_____

_____

Someone read Ephesians 6:12 and 18.

According to verse 18 what type of prayer is needed to get results?

_____

_____

_____

According to verse 12 what are our prayers for our families up against?

_____

_____

_____

Take the next few moments for several people in your group to share a need that has yet to be met, and take time praying together in faith according to Matthew 18:19-20. Commit to keep praying for the needs shared by your group.

_____

_____

_____

_____

_____

Consider singing songs of worship and praise.

Truth Talk—An Assignment of the Week

Take time this week to share with a family member or friend what you have discovered in this session. Consider saying something like:

1 "I have a new sense of God's care and compassion for me. His compassion has been very real to me, especially in regard to…

_____

The miracles of Jesus provide convincing evidences that Jesus was the perfect Lamb of God who sacrificed himself so you and I might be redeemed and justified before God. Jesus said, "Believe that I am in the Father and the Father is in me. Or at least believe because of what you have seen me do" (John 14:11). When we place our faith in Jesus we can be confident that he is the One who God accepts as a sacrifice on our behalf.

_____

_____

_____."

2 "I am amazed at God's power to intervene in our lives and the heart of compassion that prompts him to (provide / meet needs / and so on). For example…

_____

_____

_____

_____."

3 "I have a new picture of God when I come to him in prayer. I used to see God as Someone who was tapping his foot, waiting to hear what I had to say in prayer. Now I see a God who longs to be compassionate to me and can't wait for me to share my heart with him. That's made such a difference when I pray because…

_____

_____

_____

_____."

Read chapter 26 of *The Unshakable Truth* book.

||||||||||||||||||||||||||||||||||||||||||||||||||||||||||||||||||||||||||||||||||||
Close in Prayer

BEING MADE RIGHT
BEFORE GOD
= PURE JOY

Review: How did your TruthTalk assignment go this week? What was the response?

_____

_____

_____

Take a moment to again pray together for the salvation of your loved ones.

Think for a moment of an experience or time in your life that you would describe as "pure joy"—a time when you were filled with true happiness, contentment, and peace.

_____

_____

_____

Someone read the following.

> Someone has said that joy is the deeper meaning of happiness. Joy could be described then as the source or cause of happiness. Joy isn't that pleasurable feeling of the moment, but rather a deep, satisfying sense of peace and contentment regardless of life's situations. Joy can then remain intact through all of life, with or without pleasure, through ups and downs, through pain, sorrows, and losses.

Do you know of someone who in spite of trials and difficulties in life still had a sense of deep and lasting joy? Describe the person and his or her situation.

_____

_____

_____

OUR GROUP OBJECTIVE

To more deeply realize the pure joy that eternal life in Christ brings and discover better ways to share that realization with others.

Someone read Romans 3:22-28.

We are all born sinners, separated from God. Without Christ's sacrificial death and our justification before God, what would life and eternity be like? Describe a planet and a place absent of all of God's goodness and kindness.

_____

_____

_____

_____

_____

Someone has said hell is absolute aloneness with the absence of all that is good and beautiful and warm and loving. A place void of God and relationships.

Someone read John 15:11 and Romans 4:4-8.

Now describe why you have pure joy in your life since you were declared righteous before God.

_____

_____

_____

_____

_____

Someone read the following. (This is drawn from chapter 26 of *The Unshakable Truth* book.)

Your Joy Made Complete

"Long ago, even before he made the world, God loved us and chose us in Christ to be holy and without fault in his eyes. His unchanging plan has always been to adopt us into his own family by bringing us to himself through Jesus Christ. And this gave him great pleasure" (Ephesians 1:4-5). You were born dead. You were alone, abandoned, and without love because of sin. You were afraid, disconnected, and without a true family connection. But now, *if you have trusted in Jesus, you have a real family and you are somebody special.* The apostle Paul said that "God has sent the Spirit of his Son into our hearts prompting us to call out, 'Abba, Father [or Daddy]'" (Galatians 4:6).

As a result of being justified before God, his Holy Spirit enters our lives and we are adopted into his family. We not only receive his eternal life and can call God our Daddy, but "since we are his children, we will share his treasures—for everything God gives to his Son, Christ, is ours too" (Romans 8:17). Chosen, redeemed, justified, sanctified, adopted into a family, given eternal life, and willed an eternal inheritance! What more could we ask?

"King David spoke of this, describing the happiness of an undeserving sinner who is declared to be righteous:

'Oh, what joy for those whose disobedience is forgiven, whose sins are put out of sight. Yes, what joy for those whose sin is no longer counted against them by the Lord'" (Romans 4:6-8).

In effect Jesus is saying to you, "I have come to earth, demonstrated my love by giving my life for you, and I ask you to trust in me as your only solution to life, 'so that my joy may be in you and that your joy may be complete'" (John 15:11 NIV). "He [Christ] himself gives life and breath to everything, and he satisfies every need there is" (Acts 17:25). Your completion, your total joy and happiness, is found in a relationship with God as your Daddy. He didn't have to save you. But by his grace he grants you—and all of us who have placed our faith in Jesus—an adoptive relationship. We have been freed from sin, received peace of mind and heart, released from guilt, given a reason for living, and provided hope of eternal life with him. "We've been given a brand-new life and have everything to live for, including a future in heaven—and the future starts now!" (1 Peter 1:3-4 MSG).

When you experience the pure joy of a relationship with God and the hope of eternal life with him and loved ones, you want to share it. And there is no better way to convey that joy than through your personal testimony to your family first and then

00000000000000000

to others. It can be a powerful tool when developed properly. Scripture tells us, "They have defeated him [Satan] because of the blood of the Lamb and because of their testimony" (Revelation 12:11).

Your Personal Testimony

The following guidelines will help you prepare your personal testimony to share with your children, family, and friends. Read the instructions as a group, and then individually take time to write out the various elements of your own conversion story. Once you have completed it, take turns sharing what you've written with one another. Practicing on each other is good training to share it naturally with your family.

My life before knowing Christ

1. *Make your first sentence interesting and attention-getting.*

2. *Include the good elements of your life before Christ (for example, good person, athlete, achievements, moral, generous, church attender, and so on).*

3. *Identify one key problem (for example, lack of joy, lack*

of purpose, pride, wrong priorities, lack of forgiveness, reluctance to accept others, lack of compassion for others, and so on) that characterized your life before you became a Christ-follower.

4. *Show how this problem affected your life.*

   OR if you had a childhood conversion, describe your "early years."

5. *Tell of how you were provided for as a child (for example, physical needs of food and shelter were provided for by your parents or guardians).*

6. *Tell of how your need for a personal relationship with God was made evident (for example, "at the age of _____ I became aware of my spiritual need to know God because I had sinned").*

_____

_____

_____

_____

_____

||||||||||||||||||||||||||||||||||||||||||||||||||||||||||||||||||||||||||||||||||||||||||||

How I came to Christ

1. *Be specific.*

2. *Avoid confusing statements (for example, "I went forward," "I marked a card"). Also avoid "Christianese" (for example, "I was redeemed by the propitiatory, substitutionary death of the Lamb," and so on).*

3. *Talk about Christ and his work (that is, actually tell how you repented of your sin and trusted in Jesus as your sacrifice for sin and God made you his child).*

_____

_____

_____

_____

_____

||||||||||||||||||||||||||||||||||||||||||||||||||||||||||||||||||||||||||||||||||||||||||||

My life since I trusted Christ

1. *Describe how your life has changed since you accepted Christ (for example, describe how your encounter/relationship with Jesus helped you, how he has affected your actions, attitudes, and character).*

2. *Tell about your joy over how Christ dealt with your problem or, if yours was an early childhood conversion, give one positive benefit of following Christ (for example, peace, hope of eternal life, no fear of death, forgiveness of sin, purposeful life).*

3. *Be honest, positive, and realistic (for example, "Not all of my problems in this life have been eliminated").*

4. *Close with a strong, compelling conclusion.*

✓ **Avoid :**

- Clichés that are meaningless to the non-Christian, such as "blessings," "born again," "praise God," "conversion," "redeemed," "glorious," and so on.

- Vague generalities about what has happened in your life. Be specific.

- Being critical of any churches, denominations, or individuals.

- Employing too many overused catchwords such as "fantastic," "exciting," "awesome," and so on.

- Preaching. Just share your experience.

_____

_____

_____

_____

_____

✓ Now PractYour Testimony

Take turns sharing your testimony with the group as a practice. Feel free to read what you wrote as naturally as possible. With practice you will be able to share it naturally.

Truth Encounter

Someone read 1 Thessalonians 2:8.

As you are being transformed into the image of Jesus, you can count on the Holy Spirit to bring opportunities for you to share your testimony with those who do not yet know Christ as their Savior. The people you encounter will be drawn to your vulnerability and personal sharing of how God has made a difference in your life.

Have you noticed how your life has changed since trusting in Christ? Rate yourself on a scale of 1 to 10 (ten being the most change) on how God is bringing change in your life since you first trusted Christ as Savior. Then share your score with your group.

- "God displayed his love by dying for me on the cross. My gratefulness for his sacrifice has continued to increase over time. This is true of me at the level of _____ on a scale of 1 to 10."

- "As I have encountered his forgiveness I have become more forgiving of others. This is true of me at the level of _____ on a scale of 1 to 10."

- "As I have been touched by his acceptance I have become more accepting of others. This is true of me at the level of _____ on a scale of 1 to 10."

- "As I have been reassured by his compassion and care during the low moments of my life I have been motivated to care for those who are experiencing difficult times. This is true of me at the level of _____ on a scale of 1 to 10."

As a summary, complete the following sentence.

"As I have encountered Christ's (a quality of Jesus) _____, it has produced in me the desire to be more _____
_____."

Share what you have written down with your group.

TruthTalk—An Assignment of the Week

Take time this week and share your testimony with a family member or a friend. Consider saying something like:

The majority of people may believe their good deeds will persuade God to give them a place in heaven. The reality is, your death sentence, your wages of sin, is commuted, and you are redeemed and justified before God through your faith alone in Christ. And just as important, because of Christ's sacrifice and your faith in him, your status as a son or daughter of Adam

1 "During our last small group meeting, I wrote out my personal testimony of how I began my relationship with Christ. I'd like to read it to you and get your feedback. Would that be okay? (Wait for response.)

_____
_____
_____
_____."

2 "I've never really told you how I became a Christ-follower. I've been practicing how to share it with others in my small group. Can I share it with you? (Wait for response.)

_____

has changed. You are now a child of God…Your completion, your total joy and happiness, is found in a relationship with God as your Daddy.

_____
_____
_____."

3 "Jesus has made some huge differences in my life. I began my friendship with him and it's totally changed some things in me. Before Jesus, I _____ _____. And now that I have a relationship with Jesus, I…

_____
_____
_____
_____."

Read chapter 27 of *The Unshakable Truth* book.

||||||||||||||||||||||||||||||||||||||||||||||||||||||||||||||||||||||||||||||||||||||

Close in Prayer

HOW TO SHARE GOD'S PLAN WITH OTHERS

Review: How did your TruthTalk assignment go this week? What was the response?

_____

_____

_____

Keep praying for the salvation of loved ones.

In your personal testimony that you've created, you described how you became a Christ-follower. But did someone in your past explain to you simply and clearly what it took to have a relationship with God? Or did you only have a vague idea as to what you were doing? Explain.

_____

_____

_____

OUR GROUP OBJECTIVE

To examine the clear steps involved
in having a relationship with God
so we can explain it simply to
others, specifically our family.

Sometimes people make the matter of coming into a relationship with God somewhat complicated. What type of things might make coming into a relationship with God sound complicated or confusing that we want to avoid?

_____

_____

_____

Some people tend to oversimplify the plan of salvation in an attempt to make it easy for people to trust Christ. This is sometimes referred to as an "easy-believism" approach. What is the negative fallout of this approach? What is often missing in this type of presentation?

_____

_____

_____

Someone read 2 Corinthians 5:17.

Do you think it is a deterrent for people, especially young people, to be told they must turn their back on the old life (repent) and that a new life in Christ includes a changed life? Why or why not?

_____

_____

_____

If you were to paint the big picture—just a few points or steps—of what is involved in having a relationship with God, what would they be? Brainstorm within your group and come up with three to five key points that encompass a good salvation presentation.

_____

_____

_____

_____

_____

_____

_____

Someone read the following.

> There are numerous booklets and presentations from Christian organizations that can aid you in sharing a salvation message with others. A booklet from Campus Crusade for Christ is one of the most widely used tools by Christians all over the

world. It is called *Would You Like to Know God Personally?* This booklet and others like it share the big picture that

- God created us for a loving relationship with him.

- humans sinned and became separated from God.

- God's Son came to earth to sacrifice himself that humans can be restored to relationship with God.

- when we turn our back on sin (repent) and trust in Christ as our Redeemer, God promises to raise us from a dead existence without him into a Father-child relationship with him.

Following is a suggested four-point guideline for sharing with someone how to experience a relationship with God. Read the points aloud and discuss the importance of each point and how you can make it personally yours in a conversational presentation. It is a good idea to memorize the Scripture passages.

||||||||||||||||||||||||||||||||||||||||||||||||||||||||||||||||||||||||||||||||||||||||||||

Experiencing a Relationship with God Involves Four Things

1. We must recognize we have a problem with God. "No one has real understanding," the Bible says, "no one is seeking God. All have turned away from God; all have gone wrong" (Romans 3:11-12).

Recognizing our problem with God means we acknowledge that we have turned away from God and don't have enough understanding in life to decide for ourselves what is right. The Bible says it like it is: You "were once so far away from God. You were his enemies, separated from him by your evil thoughts and actions" (Colossians 1:21).

Does point 1 avoid "easy-believism" without making matters too complicated? How important is it that this generation understand they have a problem with God due to sin? Discuss.

_____

_____

_____

_____

_____

2. We must realize that Jesus Christ is our only solution.
"When people sin," the Bible says, "they earn what sin pays—death" (Romans 6:23 NCV). Our problem with God has earned us

death—separation from him. And we are totally incapable of solving that problem.

We can't just try harder to be good. You see, Jesus didn't come to earth to make bad people good; he came to earth to make dead people live. Romans 8:11 says, "The Spirit of God, who raised Jesus from the dead, lives in you. And just as he raised Christ from the dead, he will give life to your mortal body by this same Spirit living within you." So Christ is our only solution.

Recent studies reveal that 81 percent of professed Christians say the core of the Christian faith is "trying harder to follow the rules described in the Bible." How important is it to try to counter that misconception, especially to this generation? Discuss.

_____

_____

_____

_____

_____

3. We need to respond to Christ's offer to redeem us. We need to be given new life. And Jesus Christ will give us new life when we agree with him. He said:

> I am the way, the truth, and the life. No one can come to the Father except through me (John 14:6).

> You will die in your sins; for unless you believe that

I am who I say I am, you will die in your sins (John 8:24).

I am the resurrection and the life. Those who believe in me, even though they die like everyone else, will live again. They are given eternal life for believing in me and will never perish. Do you believe this? (John 11:25-26).

Do you really believe this? Are you convinced that Jesus Christ is who he said he is: the resurrection and the life, the only way to salvation, the only solution to your situation? Would you like to commit your life to him? He is ready to transform you from death to life, from separation from him to a new relationship with him. It says in John 1:12-13, "To all who believed him and accepted him, he gave the right to become children of God. They are reborn! This is not a physical birth resulting from human passion or plan—this rebirth comes from God."

How important is it that this generation believe that Jesus is the Son of God, the only way to a relationship with God? Discuss.

_____

_____

_____

_____

_____

4. You can rely on God to live in and through you. You may be dead to God because of your sins, but he is ready, as it says in Colossians 2:14, to "[cancel] the record that contained the charges against us. He took it and destroyed it by nailing it to Christ's cross."

If this prayer truly expresses the desire of your heart to begin a new life in Christ, you can pray these words to God:

- ✓ God, I recognize I have a problem with you. I have sinned against you and have gone my own way in life.

- ✓ I realize now that you are my only solution. I ask you to forgive me of all my sins. Right now I am turning away from my old life and turning to Jesus Christ as my only hope of finding a relationship with you.

- ✓ I respond right now to Jesus Christ's offer to rescue me from death. Right now I place my trust in you as my Savior and Redeemer. Right now I believe you will transform me into your child and give me an eternal relationship with you.

- ✓ I rely upon you to transfer me from death to life. You said in John 11:25 that I will be given eternal life by believing in you and that I will never die. I

believe and rely on you to transform me into your
child right now.

✓ Thank you for doing what you said you would do.
Thank you for making me your forgiven child and
bringing me into a relationship with you, the one
true God. Please live your life in and through me
every day. I pray these things in Jesus' name. Amen.

Praying a sinner's prayer in childlike faith is simple, but not
always easy to do. What often hinders this generation from taking this fourth step? Discuss.

_____

_____

_____

_____

_____

Truth Encounter

What you have just gone through is a simple gospel presentation. If there is someone in the group who has not yet made
a commitment to trust in Christ as his or her Redeemer, now
is a perfect time to do so. Is there someone willing and ready

to experience a relationship with God right now? Explore and walk through the four steps together again.

_____

_____

_____

Make the four-point guide a conversational presentation by taking turns practicing it aloud to each other. The more comfortable you become with such a presentation, the better it will be received by your family and friends.

What areas in the presentation do you find hard to explain, if any? What can be done to make it smoother to present? Discuss.

_____

_____

_____

_____

_____

Someone read 2 Corinthians 3:1-2.

Prayerfully reflect on the people in your life who might need to hear and see the gospel in your life. Ask God to reveal ways that you might both share the verbal message of the gospel and become a living letter for people around you. Pause to consider who might benefit from God's acceptance, affection, care and comfort, encouragement, and love demonstrated through you.

As I think about the people in my life, I could share a living letter of the gospel by demonstrating more of Christ's

_____ with _____ by

_____

_____

_____.

Note: In next week's session you as a group will plan an engaging mealtime with family that presents the gospel message relationally with an opportunity for your children and teenagers to trust Christ for salvation.

TruthTalk—An Assignment of the Week

Take time this week to share with a family member or friend the gospel presentation from this session. Consider saying something like:

1 "As part of an assignment from my small group I am to share the steps to having a relationship with God. Can I try it out on you? (Wait for response. Use your growth

When we receive Christ, we are assured of eternal life in heaven and joy here on earth. "God has given us eternal life, and this life is in his Son. He who has the Son has life; he who does not have the Son of God does not have life. I write these things to you who believe in the name of the Son of God so that you may know that you have eternal life" (1 John 5:11-13 NIV).

guide pages to share the gospel message.)

_____

_____

_____

_____."

2 "I've been a Christian for quite a while, but I haven't found it easy to share my faith with others. In my small group this week we were learning how to share the gospel message with others. Would you allow me to share it with you and you tell me if it really makes sense? (Wait for response. Use your session's pages to share the gospel message.)

_____

_____

_____

_____."

3 "I've been learning how God's offer of relationship is very simple, but very powerful. Can I share

with you what I'm learning? (Wait
for response).

_____

_____

_____

_____."

Review appendix A in *The Unshakable Truth* book for next
week's planning of "A Family Redemption Celebration."

||||||||||||||||||||||||||||||||||||||||||||||||||||||||||||||||||||||||||||||||||||||||||||

Close in Prayer

A FAMILY REDEMPTION CELEBRATION

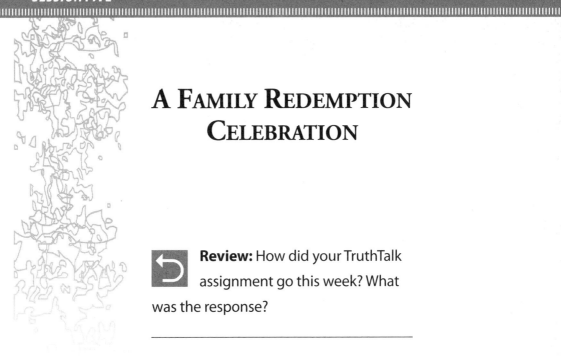

Review: How did your TruthTalk assignment go this week? What was the response?

_____

_____

_____

Someone read the following.

What Is the Redemption Celebration?

This is a family mealtime for you as a group to share the truth you have discovered about why God took on a human form and died for us. The material provided here is drawn from appendix A of *The Unshakable Truth* book.

The Redemption Celebration is a Judeo-Christian celebration modeled after the Jewish Passover *Haggadah* ("telling") that Jewish families have conducted for centuries. The traditional Jewish Passover celebrates God redeeming his people from the hands of Pharaoh and out of the land of Egypt to lead them into the Promised Land. The Passover is celebrated by Jewish families year after year as a way of passing down to their children the story of the Exodus, the story of the God of Redemption. But it is more than a story or historical event to them. The stories tell who they are, where they have come from, a depiction of a specific way of life, and a way of being in the world. Jewish parents for centuries have shared with their children that God fulfilled his promise to give them a land and make them a nation. That is why they so proudly bear the name of their forefather Israel.

You probably don't conduct a Judeo-style celebration that roots you in various meaningful historical events. Yet all of us can claim the historical and biblical roots of being the sons of

Adam and daughters of Eve. So in this Redemption Celebration we trace your heritage and that of your family back to the very first couple. We show how because of their sin we are all separated from our Creator, and how Jesus came to earth in human form, an event called the incarnation, to redeem you specifically to a relationship with him. We attempt to convey this in a dramatic yet simple story form. And at the end of the celebration we enable you to offer an invitation for family members to commit or recommit their lives to God, for he is "our Redeemer from ages past" (Isaiah 63:16).

This Redemption Celebration is best done with two or more families together. Children three years of age and up will enjoy and get something out of this celebration. This session is a time to plan and go over the details and to assign certain responsibilities for your celebration.

This celebration consists of eight elements. Walk through each of these elements with one another to practice and plan for your meal and the different readings. These elements do not include music, so your group may want to insert the singing of worship music at various times throughout the event.

1. Identify an emcee/host. Select someone in your group to be the emcee/host of the celebration the night of the meal. The guidelines for the emcee/host are found on pages 74–76.

2. "The Son of God Entered Our World" (a Scripture reading).

In your planning meeting, identify someone within the group who is willing to read this passage to begin the Redemption Celebration. The reading is found on page 77, and you have permission to photocopy that page and all the pages related to this celebration. You might ask the person to practice reading the passage aloud to the group, using the photocopied page. We encourage you to *read* these readings at the celebration rather than trying to casually relate the content. This gives your evening a sense of clarity and preciseness.

3. The "Prophet Tree." Identify someone in your group willing to present the "Prophet Tree." This person will need to follow the instructions for creating it. For practice, ask him or her to read the instructions aloud to your planning group now, found on pages 78–82.

4. The meal. Identify someone willing to take the lead to coordinate the location of the Redemption Celebration (preferably someone's home), determine the time, decide what to eat, and so on. This person is not to do all the work. He or she is to work with the members of your family group to coordinate the logistical details of the celebration listed on page 83.

5. "The Saddest Story That Could Ever Be Told: The Great Separation." Identify someone within the group who is willing to read this personalized fairy-tale-type story at the celebration. That reading is found on pages 84–87. Ask him or her to do the reading now for practice. (*Note:* The reader will need to fill in the blanks depending on his or her sex.)

6. "The Greatest Story Ever Told: The Great Redemption." Identify someone in your group willing to read this story at the celebration. This reading is found on pages 88–91. The story, of course, is real and lays the foundation for your children and youth to commit or recommit their lives to Christ. The designated reader can practice by reading to the group now.

7. "How to Experience a Relationship with God." Identify someone in your group who is willing to make a short and clear presentation of the gospel. This is to offer your children and youth the opportunity to commit or recommit their lives to Christ, the Redeemer. The designated reader can practice reading the presentation found on pages 92–95.

8. "Something to Celebrate." Identify someone in your group who is willing to conclude the Redemption Celebration by directing five people (preferably young people) to read what Jesus' coming to earth means and then close in prayer. These five readings explain the meaning of Jesus' coming to earth— and our lifelong response to our Redeemer. The designated person can practice by reading from pages 96–98.

III

Conducting the Redemption Celebration

After meeting with the families you plan to have the Redemption Celebration with, you are now ready to emcee your evening event and meal. Feel free to photocopy these pages as a reference guide to your actual celebration.

- *Introduction.* Invite everyone to be seated at the table and say, "**Tonight we are going to have a Redemption Celebration, which is a celebration of the time when God took on human form and Jesus was born into this world. And _____ (name) is going to start us off with a Scripture reading**" ("The Son of God Entered Our World").

- Immediately following the reading, have the person responsible for the Prophet Tree make his or her presentation ("The Prophet Tree").

- Announce that it is time to eat; offer a prayer for the meal.

- At the conclusion of the meal, thank all those who helped prepare it. And then say, "**Now we want to celebrate God taking on human form— which is called the incarnation. And we want to**

understand why he did that—why he came to
earth. So to begin, _____ (name) **is
going to read something. But to gain the impact
of this story, I want each young person here to
pretend that** _____ (name) **is your
actual** _____ (mother/father). **The
story is entitled 'The Saddest Story That Could
Ever Be Told: The Great Separation.'"**

- After the "Great Separation" reading, sensitively
  gauge each person's response. Ask, **"If that story
  were true, how would you feel?"**

  Then offer, **"I can tell you how I would feel; I
  would feel** _____." (Describe as honestly and vulnerably as possible how it would
  affect you.)

  Then say, **"The story that** _____
  (name) **just read shows how sad our lives would
  be if we couldn't feel each other's love. But, while
  that's just a fable, it actually parallels a real situation, a story that's absolutely true…for every
  one of us. Now** _____ (name)
  **will read 'The Greatest Story Ever Told: The Great
  Redemption.'"**

- Following the "Great Redemption" reading the

emcee says, **"Thank you, _____ (name). That is the reason God came to earth in the form of a human. It was the reason Jesus died: He wants a relationship—a close friendship connection—with you.** _____ (name) **will now explain to us how to experience that connection, a close relationship with God."**

- Following the prayer of commitment/recommitment say, **"If you prayed that prayer from the heart, a miracle has taken place, and you are now a child of God—all because of Jesus."** (Sensitively probe to see if anyone has prayed that prayer or wants to pray further—and respond accordingly. Then at the appropriate time say:) **"Let's end our time together celebrating our redemption and what we've just experienced as we respond to the very God of Redemption."** Introduce the person who is to conduct the "Something to Celebrate" presentation. Consider singing a song of praise.

- Close your Redemption Celebration in prayer.

III

The Son of God
Entered Our World
(A Scripture Reading)

God sent the angel Gabriel to Nazareth, a village in Galilee, to a virgin named Mary. She was engaged to be married to a man named Joseph, a descendant of King David. Gabriel appeared to her and said, "Greetings, favored woman! The Lord is with you!"

Confused and disturbed, Mary tried to think what the angel could mean. "'Don't be frightened, Mary," the angel told her, "for God has decided to bless you! You will become pregnant and have a son, and you are to name him Jesus. He will be very great and will be called the Son of the Most High. And the Lord God will give him the throne of his ancestor David. And he will reign over Israel forever; his Kingdom will never end!"

Mary asked the angel, "But how can I have a baby? I am a virgin."

The angel replied, "The Holy Spirit will come upon you, and the power of the Most High will overshadow you. So the baby born to you will be holy, and he will be called the Son of God."

Mary responded, "I am the Lord's servant, and I am willing to accept whatever he wants. May everything you have said come true." And then the angel left (Luke 1:26-38)…

The time came for [Mary's] baby to be born. She gave birth to her first child, a son. She wrapped him snugly in strips of cloth and laid him in a manger (Luke 2:6-7).

‖‖‖

The Prophet Tree

Instructions for Creating Your "Prophet Tree"

Before the celebration: If no one has provided you with a Prophet Tree, then take any potted houseplant or a small potted pine tree to the celebration. Prior to the celebration write or type the eight prophecies about Jesus that are listed below, including their Scripture references, on eight slips of paper approximately three by four inches. Roll the slips of paper into small four-inch rolls and tie each to a branch of the potted plant with ribbons.

‖‖

Begin the presentation

Say, **"Yes, Jesus was born in a manger. But how do we know that Jesus was truly the Son of God?"** (Pause for a possible answer.)

"Well, God gave us a way to know for certain that Jesus was his very own Son. You see, more than 400 years before Christ was born, God had his prophets foretell a lot of very specific things about Jesus. It was like identifying him by giving us his specific address. By looking back to those prophecies we know that if the information is descriptive enough, and Jesus

fits the descriptions, then we will have no doubt that Jesus was in fact God's Son.

"For example, you (name someone in the group) **are one person among more than 7 billion people on this planet. If I had the task of identifying you out of the earth's total population, I could do so by learning the answers to just eight questions. Let me ask you:**

1. What continent do you live on? _____
(African continent? European continent? North American continent? and so on)

2. What country do you live in? _____
(Canada? Germany? England? United States? and so on)

3. What province or state do you live in? _____

4. What city, borough, or town do you live in? _____

5. What street or avenue do you live on? _____

6. What is your house or apartment number? _____

7. What is your last name? _____

8. What are your first and middle names? _____

"The answers to these eight questions will enable me to separate you from the approximately 7 billion other people

alive today. In the same fashion, God gave us Jesus Christ's address. He provided us very specific information about who the Christ would be, where he would be born, and what would happen to him. And why? So that we would be convinced beyond a reasonable doubt that a Jewish man named Jesus who lived over 2000 years ago was who he claimed to be—the Son of the one true God."

||||||||||||||||||||||||||||||||||||||||||||||||||||||||||||||||||||||||||||||||||||||||||||||

Bring out the Prophet Tree

Now bring out the Prophet Tree and continue by saying:

"This is called a 'Prophet Tree.' On it we have eight prophecies about Jesus that were written down and preserved hundreds of years before he was ever born." (Select up to eight in the group—preferably young people—to untie the slips of paper from the tree and read what is inside. One person, of course, can read more than one prophecy.) They will read:

1. *He would be born in Bethlehem (Micah 5:2).*

2. *He would be born to a virgin (Isaiah 7:14).*

3. *A forerunner would announce his arrival, a "voice in the wilderness" (Isaiah 40:3).*

4. *He would ride victoriously into Jerusalem on a young donkey (Zechariah 9:9).*

5. *He would be betrayed by a friend (Psalm 41:9; Zechariah 11:12).*

6. *He would be crucified (his hands and feet would be pierced), but his bones would be left unbroken (Psalms 22:16; 34:20).*

7. *He would die (be "cut off") 483 years after the declaration to rebuild the temple in 444 BC (Daniel 9:24).*

8. *He would rise from the dead (Psalm 16:10).*

|||||||||||||||||||||||||||||||||||||||||||||||||||||||||||||||||||||||||||||||||||||||||

Could it all be a coincidence?

Continue by reading:

"Every one of these prophecies was fulfilled during Jesus' life, death, and resurrection. But couldn't that all be a coincidence? Perhaps those prophecies have been fulfilled by any number of people. Right?

"This is where the science of statistics and probabilities comes in. Professor Peter W. Stoner, in an analysis that was carefully reviewed and pronounced to be sound by the American Scientific Affiliation, states that the probability of just *eight* of those prophecies being fulfilled in one person is 1 in 10 to the seventeenth power—that's 1 in 100 quintillion.*

---

* Peter W. Stoner and Robert C. Newman, *Science Speaks* (Chicago, IL: Moody Press, 1976), 106.

"Look at it this way: If you spread 100 quintillion silver dollars across the state of Texas, they would not only cover the entire state, they would form a pile of coins two feet deep! Now, take one more silver dollar, mark it with a big red X, toss it into that pile, and stir the whole pile thoroughly.

"Then blindfold yourself, and starting at El Paso on the western border, walk the length and breadth of that enormous state, stopping just once along the way to pick up a single silver dollar out of that two-foot-deep pile…Then take off your blindfold and look at the silver dollar in your hand. What are the chances that you would have picked the marked coin out of a pile of silver dollars the size of the Lone Star State? *The same chance that one person could have fulfilled those eight prophecies in one lifetime.*

"And that's just the beginning! More than 300 prophecies in the Old Testament were fulfilled in *one person,* Jesus Christ—and all of them were made more than 400 years prior to his birth. In other words, it is completely unreasonable to imagine that the Old Testament prophecies about Jesus could have come true in one man—unless, of course, he *is*, as he himself claimed, 'the Messiah, the Son of the blessed God' (Mark 14:61-62), the One who was and is and is to come."

(The emcee thanks the presenter of the Prophet Tree, announces that it is now time to eat the meal together, and says the blessing.)

Preparing for the Redemption Celebration Meal

- **Select where to conduct your Redemption Celebration.** A person's home is preferable, depending on the size of your group and their families. Conducting the celebration simultaneously at multiple sites is an option if you have a large group.

- **Select date and time of your celebration.**

- **Decide on the meal.** Consider a potluck meal in which each family brings a dish. Decide who in your group will bring what. If you plan to conduct the celebration as an annual event you might want to identify a dish or two as a special item to always have as a traditional Redemption Celebration item.

||||||||||||||||||||||||||||||||||||||||||||||||||||||||||||||||||||||||||||||||||||

The Saddest Story That Could Ever Be Told: The Great Separation

The emcee makes an introduction: "**Now we want to celebrate the time when God took on human form—which is called the *incarnation*. And we want to understand the reason he did that—in other words, why he came to earth. To begin, _____ (name) will read us something. But to gain the impact of this story, each young person here must pretend that _____ (name of person reading the story) is your actual mother or father. This story is entitled 'The Saddest Story That Could Ever Be Told: The Great Separation.'"**

The person chosen to read stands up and begins:

"**I want you to imagine with me that once upon a time, in a land far away, I was the happiest _____ (king/queen) in all the world…the happiest _____ (king/queen), in fact, in all the history of all the _____ (kings/ queens) in all the world.**

"**This happiness was not just because I was great. It was not because I had a grand castle. It was not because I ruled a glorious kingdom. It was because on one special day, I became something even better than a great _____ (king/**

queen), **because on that day each of you were born and I
became your** _____ (father/mother).

"For months, I waited for your arrival. When you finally came
into the world, you were truly a unique, one-of-a-kind person who had never been seen before. Never in the history of
mortal time would there be another you—so distinct, so indi-
vidual, yet so connected to me.

"From the first time I scooped you up in my arms and held
you close, I wanted nothing more in all the world than to
love you, be close to you, and watch you grow to experience
all the joys of being you. You were my child, after all, and I
wanted nothing to ever come between us.

"But then…a horrible thing happened. The wicked prince of
an unhappy kingdom tried to overpower me and take control of my kingdom. But he failed because I was too strong.
So in anger and hatred, he chose to strike where he knew it
would hurt me most. He cast an evil spell over you—a great,
terrible spell.

"The evil prince's spell caused a dreadful glass wall to sur-
round you wherever you went and whatever you did. I
could still see you and hear you—for I was still the great
_____ (king/queen)—**but it trapped you**
without your knowledge. It kept you from seeing me, hear-
ing me, touching me, or even sensing that I was there.

"Thus, unless the spell could be broken, I would never again experience the pleasure, the joy, the closeness of being with you, my very own child.

"Oh, what anguish it was for me, for I could see you, but you could not see me. I saw your first steps…but you could not hear me cheering you on. I heard your first words…but they weren't spoken to me. I watched everything you did and followed you everywhere you went…but the dreadful glass wall kept you from feeling my ever-present love for you. I wanted to share everything with you—your thrill of learning to ride a bike, your relief at passing a test in school, your excitement of winning a game—but the evil spell took all that away from me.

"I was there, too, when you were hurt. When you cried, I reached out to wipe your tears away, but you never felt the touch of my hand. When you skinned your knee, I wanted to kiss it and make it better, but you didn't even know I was there. And on those nights when you would cry yourself to sleep, I heard you. I heard you cry, 'Where is my _____ (daddy/mommy)? I want my _____ (daddy/mommy).' But you couldn't hear my sobs for you.

"Oh, what a wicked spell! I would have given my kingdom—my life!—if it would break the spell and restore you to me. But it could not be, for no one on earth could break this spell.

I could only watch with broken heart, weep for you, and wait for the Spellbreaker who could reunite you with me…and bring to an end the Saddest Story That Could Ever Be Told."

||||||||||||||||||||||||||||||||||||||||||||||||||||||||||||||||||||||||||||||||||||||||||||||||

Emcee transition to next reading

After the reading, sensitively gauge each person's response. Ask, "**How would it make you feel if that story were true?**"

Then offer, "**I can tell you how I would feel; I would feel** _____." (Describe as honestly and vulnerably as possible how it would affect you.)

Then say, "**The story that** _____ (name) **just read shows how sad our lives would be if we couldn't feel each other's love. Yet while that's just a fable, it actually parallels a real situation, a story that's absolutely true…for each one of us. And** _____ (name) **now will read 'The Greatest Story Ever Told: The Great Redemption.'**"

The Greatest Story Ever Told: The Great Redemption

"In a Middle Eastern land many years ago, where a beautiful river branched out to form four other rivers, was a pristine garden. Lush tropical trees and plants produced delicious fruits of every taste and texture. A paradise of grasses and flowers under a canopy of clouds and sky painted a breathtaking canvas. Singing birds and sparkling waterfalls created a soundtrack of sheer delight. It was perfection itself, the Garden of Eden, where the first man and the first woman lived in perfect harmony with each other and with their Creator, the Trinity of God the Father, God the Son, and God the Holy Spirit.

"From the first moments of their existence, this first couple—Adam and Eve—enjoyed a close relationship with their Creator. They talked to him just as they talked to each other. They walked with him in the garden. They laughed together, sharing the delights of paradise—reveling in the gazelle's grace, the eagle's soaring strength, the sparrow's playfulness.

"They communed with God as a dear friend and loving Father, for they were a family. And through this relationship they had everything they needed. They had love, because their love came from God. They had joy, because their joy came from God. They had peace, because their peace came from God. They had no hunger, greed, fear, or pain because God's holy presence permeated the wonderful garden. They were a perfect family.

"But then something terrible happened. A rebellious angel named Lucifer plotted in hatred to ruin the perfect family and world God had created. Lucifer, who had been cast out of heaven because he wanted to rule his own kingdom without God, persuaded the first human couple that they, too, should rule their own world without God. So he deceived them into believing that they knew better than God did. He convinced them to selfishly and sinfully choose their own ways rather than trusting in God's ways.

"Adam and Eve's sinful choice to reject God and his ways formed a dreadful wall—a wall of death—that separated them from their loving Creator and Father God. *Gone* were their shared moments of intimacy and happiness. *Gone* were the moments of laughter they enjoyed together. *Gon*e was their close relationship.

"From that point on, God watched in grief and sadness as children—his children—came into the world he created without knowing him and feeling his love. He watched them every moment of the day, but they could not feel his interest. He saw them follow the sinful path of Adam and Eve, which kept every child, teenager, and adult from knowing and feeling his love.

"The perfect and holy Creator, who knew no sin, watched his sinful children—who were separated from his presence. They were now disconnected from the only source that could sustain life, love, joy, and peace. He watched as his children had to suffer the agony of war and hunger, disease and heartache, pain and suffering. Sin separated God from the cherished family he had created, and it broke his heart. But as his heart ached for his children, he already knew how he would respond.

"And this—though it is miraculous—is no fairy tale. It is absolutely true.

"God wanted to reconnect to his children and restore a relationship with them—with *you*—but God, being holy, could not relate to sin. So he devised a plan. He sent his Son into our world to become one of us—a child himself, a human baby—for you. God's own Son came to earth—in a virgin's womb, as the prophets foretold, as the shepherds learned— to cancel the curse so you could know, so you could *feel* his love for you.

"The sin of the first couple and your sin caused death, and the prince of darkness, Satan himself, held the power of death over you. Only one thing could cancel the curse of sin: A sinless human had to be willing to sacrifice himself for you. So God's Son, perfect and sinless in every way, became human. As the Bible records, 'Only as a human being could he die, and only by dying could he break the power of the Devil, who had the power of death' (Hebrews 2:14).

"He did it all for you. Though you sinned against him, he loved and accepted you. This is the meaning of redemption—to purchase you back with his blood. It shows you how much he wants a relationship with you.

"And that kind of relationship is available to anyone who responds to his offer of a never-ending, always-with-you love relationship by believing and trusting in Christ as the Son of God, your Savior, Redeemer, and friend.

"*Not* the end—but the *beginning* if you trust in Jesus the Redeemer."

Emcee:

"**Thank you,** _____ (name). **That is the reason God came to earth in the form of a human. It was the reason Jesus died—he wants to redeem you so he can have a relationship with you.** _____ (name) **will explain to us how to experience that relationship with God.**"

|||||||||||||||||||||||||||||||||||||||||||||||||||||||||||||||||||||||||||||||||||||||||||||||||||||||||||

How to Experience a Relationship with God

Trusting in the Redeemer—Jesus Christ—involves four things:

1. We must recognize we have a problem with God. "No one has real understanding," the Bible says, "no one is seeking God. All have turned away from God; all have gone wrong" (Romans 3:11-12).

Recognizing our problem with God means we acknowledge that we have turned away from God and don't have enough understanding in life to decide for ourselves what is right. The Bible says it like it is: You "were once so far away from God. You were his enemies, separated from him by your evil thoughts and actions" (Colossians 1:21).

2. We must realize that Jesus Christ is our only solution. "When people sin," the Bible says, "they earn what sin pays— death" (Romans 6:23 NCV). Our problem with God has earned us death—separation from God. And we are totally incapable of solving that problem.

We can't just try harder to be good. You see, Jesus didn't come to earth to make bad people good; he came to earth to make dead people live. Romans 8:11 says, "The Spirit of God, who raised Jesus from the dead, lives in you. And just as he raised

Christ from the dead, he will give life to your mortal body by this same Spirit living within you." So Christ is our only solution.

3. We need to respond to Christ's offer to redeem us. We need to be given new life. And Christ will give us new life when we agree with Jesus, who said:

> I am the way, the truth, and the life. No one can come to the Father except through me (John 14:6).

> You will die in your sins; for unless you believe that I am who I say I am, you will die in your sins (John 8:24).

> I am the resurrection and the life. Those who believe in me, even though they die like everyone else, will live again. They are given eternal life for believing in me and will never perish. Do you believe this? (John 11:25-26).

Do you really believe this? Are you convinced that Jesus Christ is who he said he is: the resurrection and the life, the only way to salvation, the only solution to your situation? Would you like to commit your life to him? He is ready to transform you from death to life, from separation from him to a new relationship with him. It says in John 1:12-13, "To all who believed him and accepted him, he gave the right to become children of

God. They are reborn! This is not a physical birth resulting from human passion or plan—this rebirth comes from God."

4. You can rely on God to live in and through you. You may be dead to God because of your sins, but he is ready, as it says in Colossians 2:14, to "[cancel] the record that contained the charges against us. He took it and destroyed it by nailing it to Christ's cross."

If this prayer truly expresses the desire of your heart to begin a new life in Christ, you can pray these words silently to God:

- God, I recognize I have a problem with you. I have sinned against you and have gone my own way in life.

- I realize now that you are my only solution. I ask you to forgive me of all my sins. Right now I am turning away from my old life and turning to Jesus Christ as my only hope of finding a relationship with you.

- I respond right now to Jesus Christ's offer to rescue me from death. Right now I place my trust in you as my Savior and Redeemer. Right now I believe you will transform me into your child and give me an eternal relationship with you.

- I rely upon you to transfer me from death to life.

You said in John 11:25 that I will be given eternal life by believing in you and that I will never perish. I believe and rely on you to transform me into your child right now.

- Thank you for doing what you said you would do. Thank you for making me your forgiven child and bringing me into a relationship with you, the one true God. Please live your life in and through me every day. I pray these things in Jesus' name. Amen.

The emcee makes a transition to the last reading by saying:

"If you prayed that prayer from the heart, a miracle has taken place, and you are now a child of God—all because of Jesus." (Sensitively probe to see if anyone has prayed that prayer or wants to pray further and respond accordingly. Then at the appropriate time say:) **"Let's end our time together by celebrating our new life and what we've just experienced as we respond to the very God of Redemption."** (Introduce the person who is to conduct the closing presentation, "Something to Celebrate.")

Something to Celebrate

Instructions: Photocopy and cut out the five readings on these pages, distribute them to individuals at your celebration, and ask them to take turns reading. Preferably, have young people at your meal read them. Follow the order from 1 to 5, and at the end of each reading the person will say, "That is worth celebrating." Prompt the entire group to then say, "He is worthy."

---

1. Because of Jesus, God Accepts Me Unconditionally

Like every other human being, I suffered the curse of death. I was born in sin, disconnected from God, and that broke his heart. And even though I sinned against him, he accepted me without condition. He wanted so much to have a love relationship with me that he was willing to set aside his glory, humble himself, and even go through a torturous death on a cross to redeem me, even though I didn't deserve it. Jesus coming to earth shows how passionate God is about enjoying a relationship...with me.

That is worth celebrating!
[The group responds: "He is worthy."]

---

2. Because of Jesus, God Loves Me Sacrificially

Even though I was born with a sinful nature—and added to my guilt many times by sinning myself—God solved the problem of my sin in a way that satisfied his mercy *and* his justice. "He sent his own Son in a human body…[and] destroyed sin's control over [me] by giving his Son as a sacrifice for [my] sins" (Romans 8:3). In spite of my sin, God loved me enough to sacrifice himself, and he proved it by laying down his life for me!

That is worth celebrating!
[The group responds: "He is worthy."]

3. I Must Respond by Living a Life of Devotion to God

Christ sacrificed his life for me; I can do no different for him. Romans 12:1 says, "Give your bodies to God. Let them be a living and holy sacrifice—the kind he will accept. When you think of what he has done for you, is this too much to ask?" In Exodus 34:14 it says, "You must worship no other gods, but only the LORD, for he is a God who is passionate about his relationship with you."

That is worth celebrating!
[The group responds: "He is worthy."]

4. I Must Respond by
Living a Life of Continual Prayer to God

In Hebrews 4:15-16 Jesus is called our High Priest when it says, "This High Priest of ours understands our weaknesses, for he faced all of the same temptations we do, yet he did not sin. So let us come boldly to the throne of our gracious God. There…we will find grace to help us when we need it." Prayer allows us to share our hearts and needs to God, and he is always there for us.

That is worth celebrating!
[The group responds: "He is worthy."]

5. I Must Respond by
Living a Life of Confident Faith in God

In Hebrews 12:1-2 it tells us to "run with endurance the race that God has set before us. We do this by keeping our eyes on Jesus, on whom our faith depends from start to finish." We trusted in Christ to redeem us and he did. We trust in him now to see us through the trials and difficulties of life—and he will.

That is worth celebrating!
[The group responds: "He is worthy."]

Close your Redemption Celebration in a song of worship and a prayer of thanksgiving to God for sending his Son and redeeming us.

Take the Complete Unshakable Truth® Journey!

The Unshakable Truth Journey gets to the heart of what being a true follower of Christ means and what knowing him is all about. Each five-session course is based on one of 12 core truths of the Christian faith presented in Josh and Sean McDowell's book *The Unshakable Truth®*.

The Unshakable Truth Journey is uniquely positioned for today's culture because it 1) highlights how Christianity's beliefs affect relationships, 2) promotes a relational, group context in which Christians can experience the teaching in depth, and 3) shows believers how they can live out Christianity's central truths before their community and world.

More than just a program, The Unshakable Truth Journey is a tool for long-term change and transformation!

CREATED—EXPERIENCE YOUR UNIQUE PURPOSE is devoted to the truth that God is—he exists, and he created human beings for a reason. It lays a foundation for who people are because they're God's creation, who God designed them to be, and how they can live a life of fulfillment.

INSPIRED—EXPERIENCE THE POWER OF GOD'S WORD explores the truth that God has spoken and revealed himself to humanity within the Bible. Further, he gave us his Word for a very clear purpose—to provide for us and protect us.

BROKEN—EXPERIENCE VICTORY OVER SIN examines the truth about humankind's brokenness because of original sin, humankind's ongoing problem with sin, and how instead to make right choices in life.

ACCEPTED—EXPERIENCE GOD'S UNCONDITIONAL LOVE opens up the truth about God's redemption plan. The truth that God became human establishes his unconditional acceptance of us, which defines our worth. God values us in spite of our sin. This is the basis on which we gain a high sense of worth.

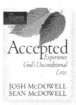

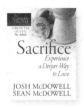

SACRIFICE—EXPERIENCE A DEEPER WAY TO LOVE digs into the truth about Christ's atonement. The truth that Christ had to die to purchase our salvation shows the true meaning of love—and how God can bring us into a right relationship with him in spite of our sin.

FORGIVEN—EXPERIENCE THE SURPRISING GRACE OF GOD explores the truth about the power of God's grace. The truth that God can offer us forgiveness in spite of our sin helps us understand how we actually obtain a relationship with him.

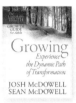

GROWING—EXPERIENCE THE DYNAMIC PATH TO TRANSFORMATION speaks to the truth about our transformed life in Christ. The truth about our transformed life in Christ defines who we are in this world and shows how we can know our purpose in life.

RESURRECTED—EXPERIENCE FREEDOM FROM THE FEAR OF DEATH focuses on the truth about Christ's resurrection. The truth that Christ rose from the grave and that his resurrection is a historical event assures us of eternal life and overcomes any fear of dying.

EMPOWERED—EXPERIENCE LIVING IN THE POWER OF THE SPIRIT covers the truth about the Trinity. The truth that God is three in one and defines how relationships work through the Holy Spirit lays the foundation for how we can experience the power of the Spirit.

PERSPECTIVE—EXPERIENCE THE WORLD THROUGH GOD'S EYES examines the truth about God's kingdom and how it defines a biblical worldview. These sessions show how to gain a biblical worldview.

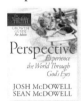

COMMUNITY—EXPERIENCE JESUS ALIVE IN HIS PEOPLE opens up the truth about the church. The truth about Christ's body—the church—provides us with our mission in life and shows us how to experience true community.

RESTORED—EXPERIENCE THE JOY OF YOUR DESTINY is devoted to the truth about the return of Christ. The truth that Jesus is coming back helps us grasp our destiny in life and gain an eternal perspective on life and death.

The Unshakable Truth Journey
Forgiven Growth Guide Evaluation Form

1. How many on average participated in your group? _____

2. Did you read all or a portion of *The Unshakable Truth* book? _____

3. Did your group leader use visual illustrations during this course? _____

4. *Group leader:* Was your experience connecting to the web and viewing the video illustrations acceptable? Explain.

   _____

   _____

5. On a scale of 1 to 10 (10 being the highest) how would you rate:

   a) the quality and usefulness of the session content? _____
   b) the responsiveness and interaction of those in your group? _____

6. To what degree did this course deepen your practical understanding of the truths it covered?

   ❏ Little   ❏ Somewhat   ❏ Rather considerably

   Please give any comments you feel would be helpful to us.

   _____

   _____

   _____

   _____

Please mail to: Josh McDowell Evaluation
                  PO Box 4126
                  Copley, OH 44321

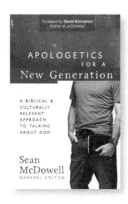

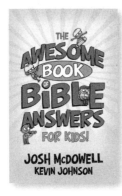

The Awesome Book of Bible Answers for Kids

Josh McDowell and Kevin Johnson

These concise, welcoming answers include key Bible verses and explorations of topics that matter most to kids ages 8 to 12: God's love; right and wrong; Jesus, the Holy Spirit, and God's Word; different beliefs and religions; church, prayer, and sharing faith. Josh and Kevin look at questions like…

- How do I know God wants to be my friend?

- Are parts of the Bible make-believe, or is everything true?

- Was Jesus a wimp?

- Why do some Christians not act like Christians?

- Can God make bad things turn out okay?

The next time a child in your life asks a good question, this practical and engaging volume will give you helpful tips and conversation ideas so you can connect with them and offer straight talk about faith in Jesus. *Includes an easy-to-use learning and conversation guide.*

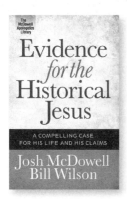

Evidence for the Historical Jesus
A Compelling Case for His Life and His Claims
Josh McDowell and Bill Wilson

After two years of intensive research, the agnostic Josh McDowell was convinced of the reliability of the historical evidence showing that Jesus of Nazareth existed and was precisely who he said he was—God in the flesh. Confronted by the living Lord, Josh accepted the offer of a relationship with him.

In *Evidence for the Historical Jesus,* Josh teams with writer-researcher Bill Wilson to provide you with a thorough analysis to document that Jesus Christ actually walked on this earth—and that the New Testament accounts are incredibly reliable in describing his life. The authors' broad-ranging investigation examines

- the writings of ancient rabbis, martyrs, and early church leaders

- the evidence of the New Testament text

- historical geography and archaeology

Detailed and incisive but accessible, this volume will help you relate to people who distort or discount Christianity and its Founder. And it will strengthen your confidence in Jesus Christ and in the Scriptures that document his words, his life, and his love.

The Unshakable Truth® church and small group resource collections are part of a unique collaboration between Harvest House Publishers and the Great Commandment Network. The Great Commandment Network is an international network of denominational partners, churches, parachurch ministries and strategic ministry leaders who are committed to the development of ongoing Great Commandment ministries worldwide as they prioritize the powerful simplicity of loving God, loving others and making disciples.

Through accredited trainers, the Great Commandment Network equips churches for ongoing relational ministry utilizing resources from the GC² Experience collection.

The GC² Experience Vision

To provide process-driven resources for a lifelong journey of spiritual formation. Every resource includes intentional opportunities to live out life-changing content within the context of loving God, loving others, and making disciples (Matthew 22:37-40; 28:19-20).

The GC² Experience Process includes:

- Experiential and transformative content. People are relationally transformed when they encounter Jesus, experience his Word, and engage in authentic community.

- Opportunities to move through a journey of...

  - Exploring Truth in the safety of relationship
  - Embracing Truth in a personal way
  - Experiencing Truth in everyday life
  - Expressing Truth through my identity as a Christ-follower

"Most of us have attended too many meetings and have gone through too many courses, only to conclude: We're leaving unchanged, and the people in our lives can see that we're unchanged. It is time to trust God for something different...a movement of life-changing transformation!"

Dr. David Ferguson
The Great Commandment Network

The Transforming Promise of
Great Commandment/Great Commission Living
www.GC2experience.com